PREFACE

This book respectfully recognizes everyone's work on the global pyramids throughout history up until today and going forward, be it authors, researchers, explorers, social media commenters, writers, readers of published and unpublished books, Masons, Egyptologists, Earth's religions, historians, website creators, online channel creators, video makers, documentary creators, radio and podcast hosts and all the teachers and people who have visited a pyramid or just thought about pyramids, because at the end of the day, it is the human consciousness that fuels the biggest discoveries throughout history.

This book is 2022 Copyright ©

John Henry Shaughnessy

1

A wee bit about the author:

40 years in power plant operations management; background in the utility fossil fuel power plants industry; utility hydro-electric plants; aero-derivative and industrial gas turbine generators. I don't profess to be a good writer, I'm an engineer and troubleshooter by trade.

Married, father of two children, with two grandchildren.

Author of "Pyramid Gravity Force".

Co Author of "There is Something About the Moon" with Wendy Salter.

Author of "Pyramids and the Great Floods," with Wendy Salter as co-researcher and editor.

Special thanks go out to my nephew, Devin Shaughnessy who worked many hours on global pyramid research so this book could happen.

My co-author, Wendy Salter, has translated my Bostonian to English to make it easier to read this third addition.

Thanks for reading.

Very rare, pre-1851 engraving of the two pyramids with colossal figures atop each. Accounted by Herodotus as being located in the center of Lake Moeris, Egypt 490 BCE.

"Man Fears time: Time fears the Pyramids", warns a 12th century Arab proverb.

After reading this book you'll understand why.

There are huge flood cycles on Earth.

To date, you may not fully understand.

This discovery outlines the water thermal cycle that manages life on Earth as we know it.

Previous societies have tried to manage this water cycle as best they can with the use of pyramids, earthen mounds and just piling up rocks and boulders on water rising up from the ground.

Noah chillin' on his yacht, otherwise known as an ark, wondering what all the people he tried to save are thinking now?

CHAPTERS

THE THEORY

There is a freshwater ocean under the Sahara Desert and under the Egyptian Pyramids; there also happens to be another freshwater ocean under the Shen pyramids in Xian, China.

There seems to be an ancient aqua vent system that connects these freshwater oceans into even larger freshwater oceans that reside in the earth's upper mantle and once they hit a certain capacity these oceans heat up and expand creating enormous pressures.

It is these oceans of subterranean water that discharge into the atmosphere under extreme pressure and high temperatures that have been referred to as the 'apocalypse', which is well documented in scripture with the flood story of Noah.

For the sake of simplicity, let's concentrate on the underground freshwater oceans located under the Egyptian Pyramids, even though pyramids are located all over the world.

Let's start at the beginning of Noah's flood: as promised by God, the rain finally came. We will skip the animals and ark part of the story for what is of grave concern here is the **source and cause** of God and Noah's flood that wiped out every living thing on land and for now let's call it "**Noah's Flood Cycle**" (**NFC** for short).

Let's start at the end of the "last" NFC. Basically, the underground fresh water ocean has now exhausted into the atmosphere leaving behind massive empty underground cavities. According to the narrative, the time that it took to empty this underground freshwater ocean was 40 days and 40 nights. The capacity of this ocean was hundreds of billions of gallons of water which is now in the atmosphere and we can safely assume that it's raining above ground and the temperatures around the globe have plummeted because the sunlight has been blocked out by cloud cover. Now, the big question is, what form of energy caused the underground water to exhaust into the atmosphere? Drum roll please!

THE HISTORY

Thermodynamics! An extraordinary reaction between the disturbed hot magma beneath the freshwater oceans and the subterranean store of water, causes the water to both heat up and become pressurized and when the critical pressure and high temperature is reached, the superheated water and steam forces its way up to the surface and shoots up miles into the atmosphere - just like on Jupiter's Moon, Europa.

Over a period of time, possibly 13 thousand years, the surface water migrates back into these empty underground ocean cavities and the whole thermodynamic process starts again to create yet another NFC. Essentially, we could be stuck in a perpetual 13 thousand year interglacial flood cycle... because we do not use the **pyramids** to manage the groundwater exhaust properly.

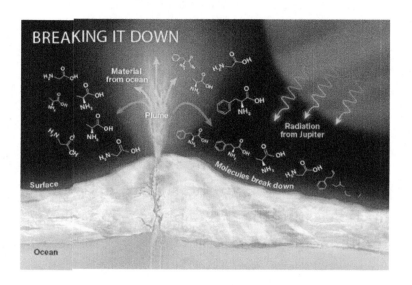

Water and steam geysers shooting miles straight up into the atmosphere from below the Earth's crust.

We would not have any idea or proof that this NFC happens other than a few scattered ancient texts on Sumerian clay tablets.

There is more to Bill Murray's Groundhog Day than meets the eye.

The fact is, if we look at this from a global society that gets wiped out and blasted into the stone age, then it obviously takes, say, several thousand years to regain the knowledge that was once had. By then, the ice core samples would have melted, erasing all data, and what we're left with is *very ancient* ice core and even those samples are suspect. That leaves only a few left over unexplained megaliths as we have today to remember and decipher our past history. In other words, we are stuck in a perpetual cycle of flood, ice age, flood, ice age, flood, ice age etc. And as a species always trying to remember our lost history.

To quote Immanuel Velikovsky, "We are a species with amnesia."

THE MECHANICS.

Now without getting dragged off into another controversial topic we will totally ignore who built the pyramid as it's just incidental.

We can agree that pyramids are on the Giza plateau and for now that's good enough.

What if I told you that many pyramids in Egypt have drilled holes, or natural vertical tube formations, that go down from the rock foundation that the pyramids were built over? These holes go down to the ceiling, or roof, of the underground ocean caverns where the freshwater oceans accumulate overtime.

Now why would anyone want to build pyramids over these massive underground pressure hydrothermal vents?

Well, (no pun intended) it would be to control the high pressure steam and water discharge. That being said, the Giza plateau pyramids are *water and steam pressure regulating relief valves* for NFC.

Why regulate it? If you can slow down NFC super-steam exhaust into the atmosphere it would help some life to survive on the planet for one, and it would reduce the planetary thermal shock that sends the planet into an ice age to say the least. There are probably a hundred more reasons to slow down the steam and water release, including using it in a beneficial technology.

The question begins with how and why the pyramids have the same function as a garden hose nozzle on a rubber hose - the most sophisticated garden hose nozzle is GP1, the Great Pyramid of Giza! These pyramids are enormous for one reason and for one reason only and that is to hold back and control the discharge of high temperature steam and water reaching tens of thousands of psi coupled with very large extreme volumes of the same.

If we take a look at the Great Pyramid of Giza, starting with the subterranean chamber being the inlet from the proposed underground freshwater oceans, we can see there is huge water erosion in the whole chamber. The deepest hole dug in the vertical tube at the bottom of the subterranean chamber is only 37 feet deep, and a large stone with holes drilled in it was also found in the subterranean chamber, resembling some sort of stone water flow check valve. Next, we will follow the flow of water up the descending passageway straight towards the outside exit door which, by the way, operates like a water check valve stone door that opens with pressure pushing from the inside of the pyramid allowing water to flow to the outside of the pyramid.

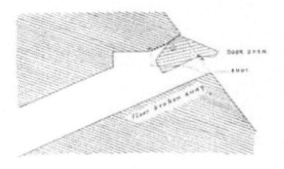

Drawing of the stone check valve located on the Great Pyramid. It opens with pressure from the inside. This is located on the descending passageway on GP1.

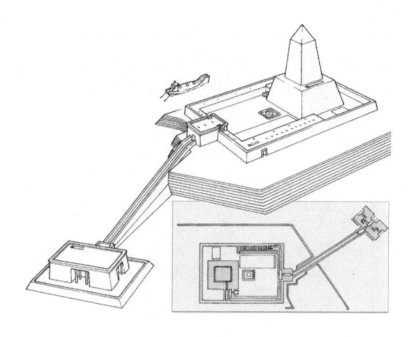

Drawing of the really old Pyramid of the Sun at Abu Ghurab, Egypt. It's all about water management.

The reason for the pyramids aligned in the so-called Orion's Belt configuration has nothing to do with the stars: the three pyramid alignment design is one of pure functionality. Ask yourself, what is it in itself? What is its nature?

The Giza plateau pyramids are geyser throttle valves that control the exhaust direction of pressurized water and steam coming up from underground oceans. The pyramids receive a vertical upsurge force of superheated water and change said force of water into a horizontal flow by discharging the water out the northern main doors of each pyramid. Because of this alignment, the horizontal geyser discharge from GP2 flows north to the west of GP1 and the horizontal geyser discharge from GP3 also flows north to the west of GP2. Essentially, the geyser northern discharge misses the other pyramids completely and heads towards the Nile. The pyramids try to control the flow and when pressures increase to critical GP3 opens first, then GP2 opens as pressure and volume increases, then GP1, the Great Pyramid of

Giza, opens last to relieve excess geyser pressure from the subterranean geyser manifold, located deep under the Giza plateau, which the three pyramids are still located over and connected to, today.

In essence, these subterranean hydrothermal geyser explosions are erratic, somewhat like a magma volcano eruption.

Underground geysers discharge from three pyramids on the Giza plateau heading towards the Nile, which runs parallel to all three pyramids; ancient causeways would direct the geyser water flow towards the Nile.

Ground penetrating radar shows ancient canals on the Giza plateau in a north south alignment, suggesting that the horizontal geyser discharge coming from all three pyramids is heading towards the Nile because the Nile river actually turns west north of the Giza plateau; one can easily speculate that the geyser water eventually flows into the Nile.

Here I am, kneeling on a ten ton stone vertical well check valve at the Pyramid of the Sun, Abu Ghurab Egypt.

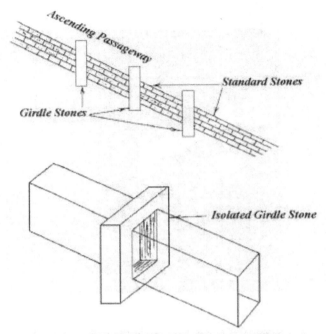

Unique Girdle Stones in The Ascending Passageway (J.P. Lepre)

Girdle stones, without a doubt, are installed to re-enforce the ascending passageway when the ascending passageway is under extreme internal pressure. A perfect design from any engineering point of view. Just pure genius. Go to milleetunetasses.com for more information.

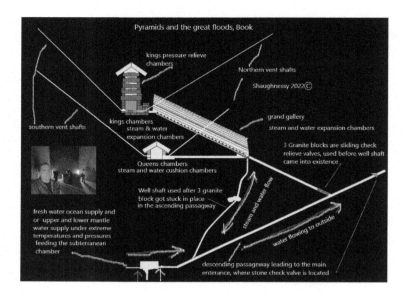

Pyramids and the great floods, Book

kings pressure relieve chambers

Northern vent shafts

Shaughnessy 2022©

southern vent shafts

kings chambers
steam & water
expansion chambers

grand gallery
steam and water expansion chambers

3 Granite blocks are sliding check relieve valves, used before well shaft came into existence

Queens chambers
steam and water cushion chambers

Well shaft used after 3 granite block got stuck in place in the ascending passagway

steam and water flow

fresh water ocean supply and or upper and lower mantle water supply under extreme temperatures and pressures feeding the subterranean chamber

water flowing to outside

descending passageway leading to the main enterance, where stone check valve is located

GP1 - The geyser water flows in both directions. Initially, the geyser water flows up the well shaft from the 'descending' passageway, then towards the Grand Gallery, ascends that passageway to the Queen's and King's chambers. As geyser pressure rises, water flows up into the five relieving chambers above the King's chamber. Ironically, the relieving chambers do relieve geyser water pressure: it seeps into the pyramid itself and many parts of the Great Pyramid have huge cavities filled with a type of quartz crystal sand. This particular type of sand does not pack down like a normal type of sand mud. It drains water without clumping up. Just more evidence that this pyramid design was set up to deal with large volumes of water.

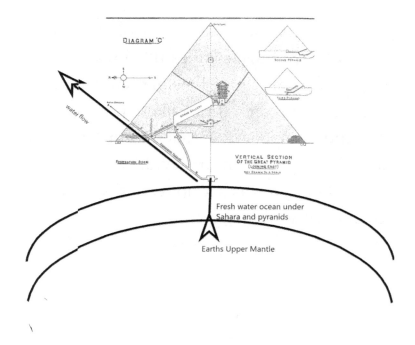

This is just a simple drawing of the source of the flood waters coming up from the earth's water cavities in the upper mantle pushing up freshwater underground oceans into hydrothermal vents under global pyramids.

"The Nubian Sandstone Aquifer System (NSAS) is the world's largest known fossil water aquifer system. It is located underground in the Eastern end of the Sahara desert and spans the political boundaries of four countries in north-eastern Africa. NSAS covers a land area spanning just over two million km2, including north-western Sudan, north-eastern Chad, south-eastern Libya, and most of Egypt. Containing an estimated 150,000 km3 of groundwater, the significance of the NSAS as a potential water resource for future development programs in these countries is extraordinary. The Great Man-Made River (GMMR) project in Libya makes use of the system, extracting substantial amounts of water from this aquifer, removing an estimated 2.4 km3 of fresh water for consumption and agriculture per year."

"The Tarim basin in China's northwestern Xinjiang province, which covers about 350,000 square miles, is one of the driest places you could imagine. Surrounded by mountains that block the passage of moist air from the ocean, it doesn't get much rainfall - less than 4 inches annually. And the shallow, silt-laden Tarim River doesn't provide much water, either.

Paradoxically, though, Chinese scientists have discovered that the Tarim basin actually has an enormous supply of water - 10 times the amount in all five of North America's Great Lakes combined, in fact. The problem is that the water in a gigantic aquifer that they describe as an underground ocean. It's too salty for the region's impoverished residents to use, but it apparently plays a role in helping to slow climate change."

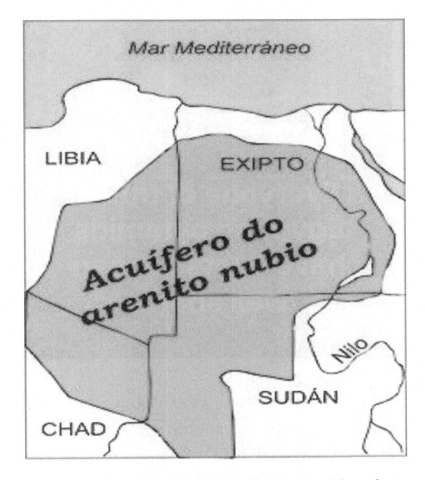

Underground Fresh Water Ocean, Acuifero do arenito nubio

Everyone of these Egyptian pyramids have subterranean well shafts

The Great Pyramid of Giza is the only pyramid where the subterranean well shaft was investigated by removing material and they only went down 37 feet because there was no end in sight. All pyramids have well shafts that connect to subterranean hydrothermal geysers.

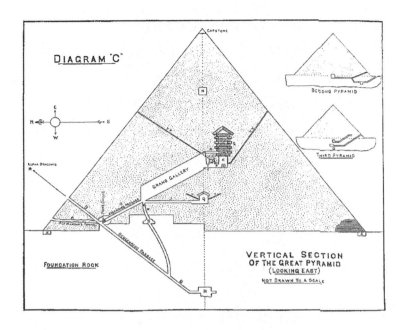

DIAGRAM "C"

SECOND PYRAMID

THIRD PYRAMID

VERTICAL SECTION
OF THE GREAT PYRAMID
(LOOKING EAST)
NOT DRAWN TO A SCALE

FOUNDATION ROCK

The ascending passageway has granite plugs blocking the connection to the descending passageway, the well shaft connects the ascending and descending passageways where steam and water both flow up to the Queen's chamber, up the Grand Gallery, up to the Portcullis chamber and finally to the Kings chamber. The functionality of the King and Queen's chambers and the Grand

Gallery is as expansion chambers, or steam cushion valves. When the Great Pyramid was first built the Queen's chamber was the highest expansion chamber in the pyramid equipped with a Portcullis chamber; the Grand Gallery and two air shafts during this time of operation are the same as the future King's chamber would be. The shafts were, and still are, relief valves, or over pressurization vents.

The 5" of stone left behind in the recessed hole connecting to the vent shafts are blow-out stone diaphragms. The same techniques are used today to prevent over pressurization of a space or closed vessel. In essence, the shafts were set up as pressure relief vents. Once the stone diaphragms blew out the high pressure would exhaust to the outside of the pyramid.

The Portcullis chambers with doors acted like baffles to lower the water and steam flow volumes heading towards the King's chamber. There is extensive water erosion at the end of the Grand Gallery leading into the Portcullis chamber that they call the 'big step' and more erosion on the Portcullis doorway top opening, seen when entering the King's chamber.

The ceiling of the Grand Gallery has pitched tiles that allow water to flow to the edge of the tile and drip off.

I think you're starting to get the picture as to the true purpose for the Great pyramid of Giza. It was designed and built to control a type of water volcano, a type of volcano that only exhausts super high temperature water and steam.

GP2 - If you look at the stone configuration leading straight up from its subterranean chamber, you can see the enormous erosion and damage caused by the discharge of the water and steam pressure blasting away at these stones. In one drawing they look like they have been tossed around like toy blocks.

WHEN IT GOES WRONG

GP3 – This pyramid also has chambers and portcullises that were used to manage the enormous pressures and water flows.

Let's talk about GP3, and that enormous gash in the northern face above the main entrance. The story goes that during the 12th century CE, a son of the then renowned Saladin Aziz, who was Governor of Aleppo from 1183 to 1186, who also returned to administer Egypt during the 3rd and 5th crusades, led a Muslim army against the pyramid of Menkaure to dismantle it and to prove superiority of Islam. As the story goes, someone did some quick calculations after eight months of intense labor and figured they would run out of money at the pace they were going, and abandoned the attack. Here is where I disagree with this story: anyone with half a brain who was tasked with dismantling a pyramid would just start pushing the blocks off the top of the pyramid, but what we see is a huge gouge in the center of Menkaure's pyramid.

Over the main entrance doorway, the gouge can be seen. My investigation has led me to believe that it was caused by internal over-pressurization that blew out the pyramid face and not a manmade gouge after all.

"He who controls the present, controls the future and controls the past."

Menkaure Pyramid on next page.

GP4 - Now let's move up north to Abu Ruwash, 8 miles north-east of Cairo, and see what happened to GP4! The entire pyramid is gone! This is a major problem because the hole that taps into the underground fresh water ocean in GP4's subterranean chamber has no way of throttling the discharge when the next NFC starts. The high temperature steam and water is just going to blow straight into the atmosphere taking the least path of resistance, whereas the other pyramids will manage the water from the underground freshwater eruption.

It's entirely possible that this pyramid got destroyed trying to throttle down the discharge in the previous event.

SUBTERRANEAN WORLD

It's entirely possible that the holes or tubes that connect the surface to the underground fresh water ocean happened naturally as there are many cooling vents located all over the planet. I hinted before that someone may have drilled them out, but at this point it really is not important who or how the tubes or holes came to be. What is of primary importance is that we rebuild GP4 as soon as possible so there are 4 pyramids working to throttle down the discharge.

It's not going to be easy to sell this technology to the people in charge, but the current state of the pyramids in all of Egypt is one of severe damage and unsealed, which means that when the next NFC water eruption happens the superheated water and steam is just going to blast straight out into the atmosphere with no restraint at all. The planet will shut down extremely fast destroying much more life than need be.

LEGENDS OF FLOODS

Zecharia Sitchen's work on the Sumerian cuneiform tablets and the revealing of the Annunaki story, tells of a flood story.

Enki was on his spaceship in lower orbit around Earth during the flood. They were out of food and so they came closer. Sitchin writes that the Anunnaki could smell the food the humans were cooking (more like rotting carcasses - a topic for another discussion). They decided to land on Earth and seek out the humans.

Every continent has a flood story attached to that particular geographical location. In South America during the Ancient Mayan Empire period, many hieroglyphs that have survived show people trying to manage water flowing up from under them while they were building pyramids! (You can't make this stuff up!)

Flood Tablet Epic of Gilgamesh

PLUMBING LOGISTICS.

Back to the subterranean chamber and the function of the other chambers in pyramids. Having been in the modern utility power plant business in New England, USA, for over 40 years, there is one problem I am familiar with. It is something called 'water hammering' and it's when water flows down a pipe at high speed but then suddenly stops when it meets a void. The energy force from the water pressure that has been halted can be strong enough to destroy equipment and pipelines in seconds.

Water is dense and heavy: imagine you have thirty gallons of water flowing at fifty miles per hour in a pipe line - the weight of that water is 250 pounds and it comes to an instant stop. That's an enormous amount of force for a pipeline and pipe hangers to absorb. Now let's multiply that to a magnitude of ten thousand times higher in weight and speed and you'll need a six million ton pyramid to absorb this energy.

In the plumbing industry there is a simple device called an 'air cushion chamber'. It is usually an empty piece of pipe set at a right angle to the water pipeline, that is installed vertically, usually a foot or two long. This empty pipe is the 'air cushion' as it always has air trapped inside.

Many times, you'll see these 'air cushion chambers' on the hot and cold water supply lines going to a washing machine. This is due to the fact that washing machines have electric solenoid valves that open and close extremely fast, which causes undesirable water hammering in the pipes and will eventually cause a water leak over time.

The Great Pyramid of Giza – the King & Queen chambers, and the Grand Gallery, are 'air cushion chambers' for the superheated water and steam coming up from the well shaft and through the descending passageway at great speed and pressure and designed for the same purpose - to lower the occurrence of water hammering effects in the internal chambers and passageways of the pyramid.

This high flow and high pressure water and steam condition, on entering the pyramid, takes an immediate right-angled turn up the descending passageway. Now the flow is causing compression in the air pressure inside the pyramid passageways and chambers, which are now acting like giant 'air cushioning chambers' as they were originally designed to do.

The force of water continues until it smashes into the stone entrance door and pushes in open, allowing the discharge of the now depressurized water to flow outside. As the flow continues under pressure, it will fill the Queen's chamber and the Grand Gallery and eventually the into the King's chamber. By this time the so-called air vents are still sealed and the recesses inside the granite blocks have not been breached yet. Note that these notched plunged cuts go into the granite blocks but stop 5" before going all the way through into the chambers. (See diagram below)

Shaughnessy

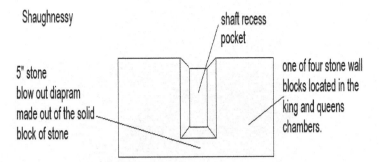

shaft recess pocket

5" stone
blow out diapram
made out of the solid
block of stone

one of four stone wall
blocks located in the
king and queens
chambers.

Shaft block cut away side top view showing plunge cut from back side where stone shaft or vent slides in, also the remaining 5" located on the chamber side which is a blow out diafram that acts like a releive valve when maximum alowable pressure is reached it cracks and disintergrates allowing high preasure in the king or queens chambers to escape out the shaft to prevent damage to the king and queen chambers,

OOPOs
Out of place objects.

The infamous 'sarcophagus' located in the King's chamber was brought into the pyramid through the so-called 'Al Mamun's tunnel', sometime after 833 AD, I'm speculating here, as an *unbroken* sarcophagus would not make the turn from Al Mamun's tunnel into the ascending passageway and would not fit; that said, a *broken* sarcophagus with a corner missing would make the turn and fit easily. And as for the other pyramids with sarcophaguses in them, I believe the same is true - they were placed in them long after the pyramids were built.

During the 26th Dynasty, the beginning of the Late Period in Egypt (7th – 6th century BC), there were a lot of renovations carried out in Egypt and that's when the Valley of the Kings' tombs were created. It's possible that Al Mamun's tunnel may have been made then, and the sarcophagus, or granite box, was brought up into the King's chamber for the then pharaoh who then decided not to use the Great Pyramid as his final resting place.

King's Chamber, northern shaft.

Southern shaft in King's chamber with a fan installed to remove humidity from humans.

TECHNOLOGY OLD AND NEW

This same technology is used today as a relief valve, or blow-out port, or blow-off diaphragm on a pressure vessel: it's fool-proof, tried and tested and lasts a long time.

Going full circle, the engineers that built the King and Queen's chambers calculated the maximum allowable working pressure of the chambers, thus calculating the tensile strength of five inches thickness of granite in the King's chamber and the five inches thickness of limestone in the Queen's chamber - five inches being the approximate thickness on the stone left behind the recess. We know now that for a 5 inch piece of granite to fail and blow out towards the shaft, the pressure required is in the thousands of psi. With this number we can calculate *the maximum allowable working pressure* of the

King's chamber designed by its engineers. We can also use the same technique to figure out the maximum allowable working pressure [MAWP] of the Queen's chamber, when we figure out the critical pressure of a five inch thick piece of limestone, width of eight inches and a height of 9 inches.

8 x 9 x 5 = MAWP.

On the second rebuild of the GP1 the Queen's chamber was sealed off and decommissioned along with her two shafts, where doors were place at the top ends of the shafts. The world got a picture of said doors from the Rudolph Gantenbrinks' robot *Upuaut*, a truly amazing achievement by everyone involved (which, by the way, I could not be writing about now without this work).

Obviously, the King's chamber had hit the high pressure limit because both blow-out ports were opened. In other words, the two shafts were open when explorers in the 1800s started to draw pictures and record the state of the interior of the pyramids in writing.

THE MISSING PYRAMID

Let's look at the missing pyramid at Abu Ruwash, eight miles NW of Cairo (See page 31). It's got descending passageways, subterranean chambers, a base foot print the size of GP3, but the pyramid is completely destroyed. Ancient stories tell us that the pyramid exploded because of some kind of cataclysm and the remaining pyramid stones were at some point carted off to build Cairo to the tune of three hundred camels a day.

From my point of view, we have another possible tube that goes down to the underground freshwater ocean that needs to have a pyramid built over it to manage the discharge of this superheated water and steam. Do you see what we are up against?

Another opened pit that looks to be another possible foundation to a blown up pyramid, is Zawyet El-Aryan. This place had an oval red granite polished sarcophagus that is now being used as a trash dump!

It's been well documented that there are aqueducts or tunnels all over the Giza plateau. I'm theorizing that there are thermal vents located in Saqqara, Abusir, Dashur, Medun, as well as on the Giza plateau. And pyramids are built on top of all of these vent tubes that connect to the underground fresh water oceans. The aqueducts or tunnels that connect to the pyramids are for **the express purpose of reducing the direct discharge of superheated steam and water into the atmosphere, which in turn will stop an instant ice age from happening**. I am also open to the idea mentioned above that vertical holes might also have been bored down into the earth, by humans, just like we do today to drill for oil or ground water, as there is evidence all over Egypt of advanced drilling technology.

Now that we know that all of the pyramids discharge the subterranean superheated water and steam, or geysers, to the outside of the pyramid via passageways in a **horizontal** direction, thereby stopping the superheated water and steam blasting hundreds of miles straight up directly into the atmosphere, obviously we a dealing with a very highly advanced technological reducing-valve system which will **reduce the thermal crash of the environment.**

WHAT'S NEXT?

Where are we right now when it comes to controlling the next NFC event? We are totally screwed! We couldn't be in a worse place right now even if we tried. Every pyramid on Earth is opened up with stone check valves blocked, opened or missing altogether. GP1 has a bypass tunnel going around the main entrance. At least two pyramids are missing altogether in Egypt alone and to make things even worse, the pyramid community has been hijacked by the tourism industry, not to mention the uphill battle to re-educate the intellectually challenged academic, history and archaeology crowd.

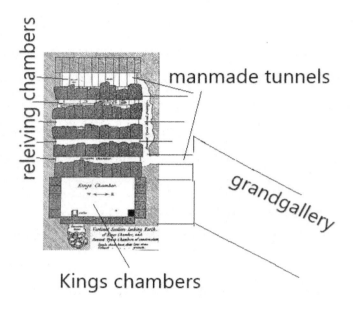

relieving chambers

manmade tunnels

grandgallery

Kings chambers

The king's relieving chambers have been compromised by - you guessed it - humans tunneling into them! If the relieving chambers were exposed to the enormous pressures of a blow-out, the entire pyramid would explode, just like the one at Abu Ruwash.

THE DRIVER BEHIND THE WHEEL

What drives and governs the NFC cycle?
After the subterranean fresh water oceans heat up and exhaust into the atmosphere, the underground freshwater caverns are emptied, which drives the planet into an instant ice age, relatively speaking. The north and south poles begin to accumulate ice and head towards what we call the glacial maximum. Once the glacial maximum has been achieved, the planet slowly moves through its cycles and heads back to the interglacial period, where the ice of the polar caps begins to melt back to liquid water and flow back into the world's oceans. At this point the flesh water ocean caverns begin to fill up again with the slow process of water migration. The salt gets trapped in the land mass and filters out the salt from the ocean water.

This process to refill the underground freshwater oceans usually takes thirteen thousand years, heading to what I call the **water maximum** on the planet, thus the whole ice age process starts over again when the freshwater oceans heat up and discharge back into the atmosphere.

Like I mentioned before, Earth could actually be stuck in a perpetual thirteen thousand ice age-and-water age; or even less, like a seventy five hundred year ice-age-and-water age, with humans never breaking out of this climate trap; it's one big pendulum swinging from the big freeze to the great flood and back again, leaving traumatized humans too busy surviving to never achieve galactic travel technology.

Earth hasn't had a massive and catastrophic steam and water discharge into the atmosphere for, I'm guessing, six thousand to thirteen thousand years.

THE HOW, WHEN AND WHERE

I think I have opened up the possibility of yet another potential cause to explain the Younger Dryas – the event where a sudden and unexpected mini ice age occurred some 12,900 and 11,600 years ago.

Unexpected things happen, like in 2018 when millions of tons of molten lava came flowing out of the Kilauea volcano, the Hawaiian 'hot spot', for thirty days straight. Four years ago, after only two months of earthquakes and small eruptions, Mount St Helens erupted with cataclysmic violence. We see the dramatic geyser 'Old Faithful' in Yellowstone National Park blast out a column of steam and hot water every hour like clockwork. 'Steamboat Geyser', also in Yellowstone N. P., erupts infrequently, with events occurring many months to many years apart but has risen to 400 feet high and has been extremely active since March of 2018. With those four vents in mind we can easily see that Earth can produce the right conditions for sudden multiple venting above ground.

A hot water spring, also known as a hydrothermal vent, is a natural discharge of hot water out of the earth. Such hot springs normally occur in areas where underground water passes through hot igneous rock. They can form pools, geysers or fumaroles. There are steaming hydrothermal vents in the floor of every ocean on earth, especially around the Pacific 'Ring of Fire'. And it is when fire (magma) and water come together we see these explosive superheated occurrences.

The root cause for Noah's flood and recurring ice ages is not above ground, but deep in the upper mantle in what is called the 'Transition Zone'. At this depth, rising magma can break through the vast oceans of water stored under immense pressure in a layer of crystalline rock, called 'Ringwoodite'.

For the full article on this discovery please refer to this site blog.crystalrockstar.com/ or search "Discovering Underground Oceans Through Ringwoodite Crystals"

Underground freshwater oceans also refill when rising ocean levels force a downward filtration. Oceans rise and fall in cycles over time, and a dramatic rise comes from melting glaciers and polar ice-caps. The added depth and pressure pushes more ocean water through the land mass to raise the volume in the freshwater underground oceans filling caverns and tunnel networks.

And even more earth changes like the rise of the north and south polar land caps, due to loss of ice weight and the contraction of the plate tectonic boundaries between the tropics of Cancer and Capricorn, redistributes the hot magma currents to a critical point where the underground freshwater ocean begins heating up. With heat comes expansion and pressure changes. At a critical point of heat and pressure the water turns to steam and seeks an escape route to be released.

The heat and pressures rise and keep rising, coupled with the compression from subterranean crust and plate movement. My guess at the pressure reached is in the neighborhood of 5000 to 7000 psi or even more. In the Gulf of Mexico oil rig disaster of 2010, in the oil well-head manifold, the pressure at the Deepwater Horizon that blew apart on the Gulf floor was over 7000 psi!

Now we can understand why pyramids need to be so massive.

However, it is now known that the pressure deep down at the Transition Zone, at 430 km deep, is up to 3 million psi!

It's seems obvious once you just add thermodynamics into the equation; and scientists have been scratching their heads for years trying to solve this riddle – where did Noah's flood water come from... before it started to rain?

In the biblical account of Noah's Flood, the narrator describes how the flood water "came up from the deep" and then it rained and rained for 40 days and 40 nights.

"All the **fountains of the great deep** were broken up, and the windows of heaven were opened." Genesis Ch 7: v 11

When the geysers, **fountains of the great deep,** fire off into the atmosphere, the steam obviously cools to rain down as water.

And how much water are we talking about?

"Fifteen cubits [more than 20 feet] upward did the waters prevail; and the mountains were covered."
Genesis Ch 7: v 20

It is uncertain if this is a sea-water level rise, or the final depth above the covered mountains, in that location.

At climatecentral.org/ much is written on a prospective 20 foot sea level rise, blaming a 2C degree temperature rise, with the potential loss of 150 million people from currently inhabited land.

Advanced technology and recent papers published have proven that a vast quantity of water is located deep underground. It's only a matter of time that, in certain locations, underground oceans will be heating up and building up enormous amounts of pressure before it pushes back up to the surface. Let's hope this pressurized flow ends up going in the same directional location - under the pyramids -so we can at least have a chance to throttle or regulate this hydrothermal explosion before it goes into the atmosphere and causes another 40 days and 40 nights of raining deluge, which will end up pushing Earth into a deep ice age overnight, relatively speaking.

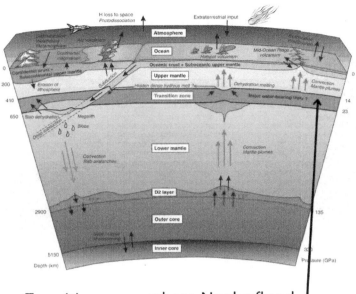

Transition zone where Noahs flood
water is located

JUPITER'S MOON

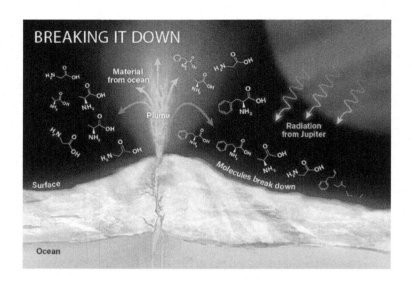

Europa is a moon of Jupiter covered in water; it has constant water geysers that shoot up **200 KM,** or 125 miles, above the frozen surface. While Europa is only a quarter the size of the Earth, one could easily deduce that the Earth's core, having four times the heat, could shoot water geysers hundreds of miles into the sky above its surface also.

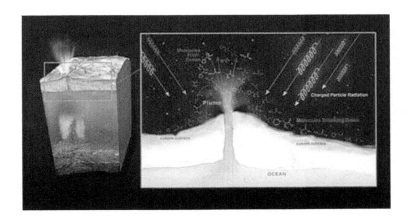

Another display of the awesome power of water geysers spraying 125 miles up into the atmosphere of Europa. Without a Transition Zone or upper and lower mantle on Europa, the explosive force of geysers is incredible. When the Earth's Transition Zone fractures to release billions of gallons of water the geysers on Earth could go hundreds of miles straight up into the atmosphere.

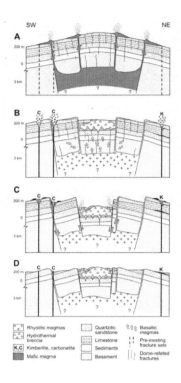

SW   NE

A

200 m

0

3 km

? ?

B

C C   K

200 m

0

3 km

? ?

C

C C   K

200 m

0

3 km

? ?

D

C C   K

200 m

0

3 km

? ? ?

Rhyolitic magmas	Quartzitic sandstone	Basaltic magmas
Hydrothermal breccia	Limestone	Pre-existing fracture sets
Kimberlite, carbonatite	Sediments	Dome-related fractures
Mafic magma	Basement	

Subterranean freshwater plug mechanics that
are self-sealing miles below the surface of the
Earth.

74

GIZA'S PLATEAU

Satellite imagery has detected underground caves connecting the Giza plateau pyramids. With this in mind, I formulated my theory that the pyramids are a multiple pressure reducing device built with the sole purpose of reducing the vast amount of high pressure steam and water emitted from deep geysers to prevent mega-fountains of superheated steam from shooting into the sky. It would also stand to reason that one large primordial vent tube is rising up from the underground freshwater ocean that connects directly into these caves or cavern system like a three-way manifold, distributing this enormous high pressure steam and water flow to the three pyramids of the Giza plateau which, from an engineering point of view, helps to distribute the pressure equally to the pyramids and keeps the structural integrity intact inside the pyramids.

Seeing that the Great Pyramids sit on a high plateau, the Giza plateau, one can speculate that an ancient vent does indeed exist underneath the plateau. Furthermore, was the explosive force that actually pushed the Giza plateau up to that height we see today a mega-geyser of superheated water?

Don't you find it strange that all the Anunnaki tablets that recorded the flood and what caused it - about 7 of them all together - are either missing or destroyed? Obviously someone has been working very hard to keep the cause of the great recurring floods a big secret.

Well let's set the record straight and free humanity from the bondage of ignorance.

I always knew there was a mechanism that shut the planet down or triggered an ice age. Milutin Milankovitch is the leading theorist on how ice ages begin on Earth. All of his theories are contingent on *external* forces on the planet. He proposes the sun's discharging output energy lowers (solar minimum) or Earth's orbital path around the sun changes from an elliptic shape to a circular shape, (but that's been rejected as the planet would still receive the same amount of energy on both orbits); finally he suggests it is the Earth's changing tilt that would lower thermal energy if, say, it went to 19.4 degrees.

A 3rd century Greek bible text tells of Noah's *ark* but, correctly translated, it should read Noah's *pyramid*. Why do you suppose they are making a connection between an ark and a pyramid? It's becoming more and more obvious to me that there has been a concerted effort to obscure a narrative because it was not understood, or it was feared, and that narrative is the recurring flood and the mechanics behind said flood.

Nostradamus knew…he saw
"A Horrible Undoing of People and Animals"
(Nostradamus Quatrain 62)

WHAT WE KNOW

We are left with a few theories as to what water sources supply the pyramids on the Giza Plateau.

1. There is an underground freshwater ocean located under the Sahara desert and the Giza plateau,
2. The planet Earth is in a constant state of change
3. Compression and heat from the mantle could easily be the forces that could heat and build pressure on this underground fresh water ocean and cause it to exhaust into the ancient vent tubes and caverns connecting to subterranean chambers of the three pyramids on the Giza plateau.
4. There could be a much more destructive force behind the Noah

Flood Cycle. This one is the most frightening: the Wrath of God!

5. Recent discoveries have identified enormous water sources located between the upper and lower mantle, called the Transition Zone. Page 69.

6. Science shows that there are channels located along the subduction zones, where water can be drawn down through the upper mantel into the Transition Zone.

7. *Ringwoodite* is a crystalline rock layer in the Transition Zone that is capable of storing enough water to "…easily cover the entire planet Earth with water submerging the tallest of mountains"

8. What goes down can also go up!

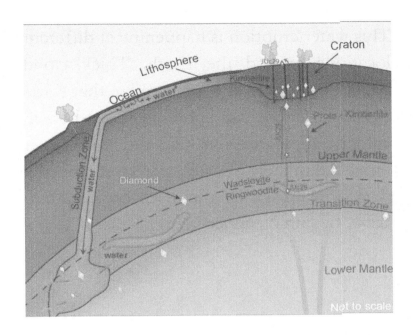

A divided firmament to a single firmament. Ice caps melt to water; this water flows into the oceans; the oceans drain down through the upper mantle into the Transition Zone until saturation point; water eruption phase happens sending water up through the upper mantle and out hundreds of miles into the atmosphere.

This water eruption is happening at different locations around the Earth. Thick cloud cover develops in the atmosphere that starts to block out the sun light and this ushers in colder temperatures around the globe, over time. Ultimately Earth starts entering a period where glaciers and ice caps start to grow, beginning an ice age.

THE DIAMOND CLUE

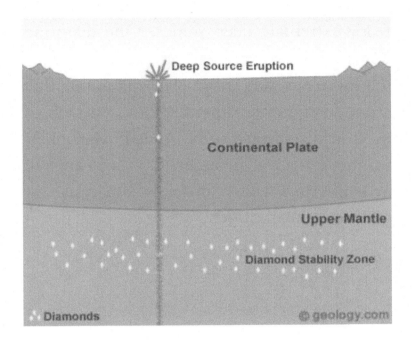

De Beers, a diamond mine in South Africa, supports the theory that material flows up to the surface from the Wadsleyite and Ringwoodite crystal rock layers called the Transition Zone. As mentioned earlier, it was evidence from this depth that brought us knowledge of the capacity for Ringwoodite to hold vast amounts of water. Diamonds are formed in the Transition Zone but are mined from extremely deep mines. One diamond was found to contain Ringwoodite, and so the discovery was made. The diamonds that arrive in the upper mantle, close enough to the Earth's surface to be mined, were likely to have been brought up by ancient hydrothermal vents, possibly the cause of previous global floods.

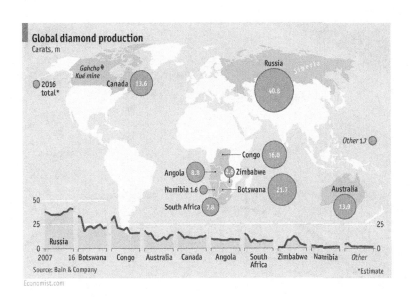

Global diamond production
Carats, m

2016 total*

Gahcho Kué mine

Canada 13.6

Russia 40.8

Siberia

Other 1.7

Congo 16.0

Angola 8.8

Zimbabwe

Namibia 1.6

Botswana 21.7

Australia 13.9

South Africa 7.8

50

25

Russia

0

2007 16 Botswana Congo Australia Canada Angola South Africa Zimbabwe Namibia Other

25

0

Source: Bain & Company

*Estimate

Economist.com

85

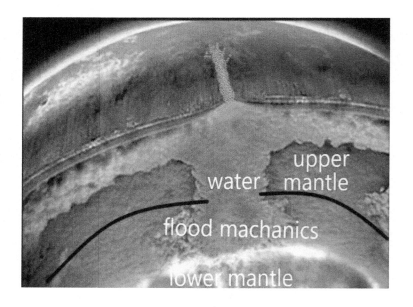

Image shows a possible change from magma erupting out of the earth, to water erupting out of the earth - Noah's Flood Cycle mechanics.

THE FIRMAMENT

When God made the world it was covered in water and he split the water dividing it in two, one layer of water was above the firmament and the second layer of water was under the firmament:

6"And God said, 'Let there be a firmament in the midst of the waters, and let it divide the waters from the waters."
7"And God made the firmament, and divided the waters which were under the firmament from the waters which were above the firmament." Genesis Ch 1 v 6-7

This word, 'firmament' seems to be both heaven and earth, but in this case the waters were both under and above the firmament so maybe the firmament is the Earth's crust.

PYRAMIDS

There is nothing but cavities and passageways inside the pyramids – no coffins, no artefacts, no statues, no paintings, no writing: they were **not tombs**! No-one has come up with a working theory on what they were made for, but now I am proposing that they had a very serious function – to save the world from another devastating flood by regulating the mega-geysers from hell itself, the underworld, the world of the dead – the deep earth. They were built with absolute precision to withstand unimaginable pressures and volumes of superheated steam and water.

It's time to go out on the proverbial limb: with this new breakthrough of understanding, we can deduce that most of the large pyramids built around the world may have been used to plug an underground pressure-water-discharge-tube to head off God's biblical floods. To super simplify it, pyramids are no more than a cork in a wine bottle. But there are many pyramids located around the world, even the large earthen types found in Bosnia, that have dry tunnels, and some with flowing water in tunnels.

The Pyramid of the Sun in Mexico has an original vent tube under it and in the upper layers of the Pyramid of the Sun there was an enormous 10 inch thick slab of mica. I'm sure if they excavated lower into the pyramid they would find more slabs of mica which, by the way, was somehow transported from Chile, 2000 miles away. In addition to the above, the significance of mica is its ability to withstand high pressure water and extreme high temperatures and is still used today in nuclear power plants and fossil fuel power plants. It is used to protect equipment and to be able to view actual physical water levels in nuclear reactors and in steam boiler drums operating up to 3000 psi. This top layer, which was reported to be one piece thirty feet by thirty feet square, was removed and shipped to England to be used in the electrical industry. We can safely assume that this Pyramid of the Sun in Mexico will not be able to hold back the enormous water pressure and temperatures next time around unless we install another slab of steel or mica.

Another anomaly is the other Pyramid of the Sun, located in Bosnia. A discovery under said pyramid suggests that there is a huge steel plate located under this pyramid - another technique to check a release of uncontrolled water. As you can see, the high pressure and high temperature evidence snowball is rolling, getting larger and larger.

Many of the catastrophic conditions that the Earth goes through are still under investigation but we have geological evidence of great floods recurring around the world. In all cases it ends up with 99 per cent of life on land succumbing to the waters and perishing. Not a real happy ending.

GEO-HYRO-THERMAL MANAGEMENT.

There is no end to the questions when it comes to ancient floods. Now that this can of worms has been opened, or the proverbial Pandora's Box has been unlocked, there is something else. I also have to consider that these high pressure and high temperature water exhaust geysers causing floods around the Earth might be of a much older time on Earth - a much, much older and ancient time on Earth, not relevant for the environment we know today. However, water is continually recycling and renewing and cycles of environmental change continue as we speak.

Ideally, the best place to have an unregulated discharge of water from the earth's upper mantle would be to have it discharge into the ocean. This way the high pressure steam would be mixed with cold ocean water that would condense the steam back to water before it goes into the atmosphere, and the environmental impact would be minimal. If these mega-geysers exhaust themselves in the middle of a populated city, it would be a very different story and then my theory comes sharply into focus as to why the pyramids are built all over the Earth.

We have Ancient Maya carvings showing them dealing with and living in a flood environment; this particular picture actually shows them building a pyramid where they are completely inundated with water. See the waves running all around the picture?

It makes total and complete sense to cover, plug and regulate every known water-steam geyser hole on land with giant pyramids or huge foundations. This in effect would redirect the billions of gallons of water into the ocean and lower the amount of moisture going into the atmosphere thus lowering the thermal shock that would drive the planet into an ice age. The planet is still going to go into an ice age because said thermal energy is going to heat up the world's ocean eventually and liberate more moisture in the air causing a complete cloud effect covering the earth reflecting sunlight driving the planet into the next ice age, but slowly and without a devastating shock to life for humans and creatures on land in a catastrophic way.

BEING PREPARED

It seems that we are in an hourglass filled with water, not sand, and it's a well-designed regulatory system to protect not only life on the planet but the planet itself. Earth is either warming up or cooling down, constantly and cyclically. That's the best thermostat planets of our type have, even if it causes some uncomfortable and scary disruptions for us humans.

Now why do you suppose a rather large wooden ship was buried at the side of the Great Pyramid? It's presumed that it's for the pharaoh's pleasure, in his lifetime or his afterlife. Is it possible that mankind can't remember its past and someone with a distant memory had to bury a big clue - a ship - for their future human family? Obviously, we are trapped in a vicious cycle of ice age and water age, and we don't seem to take it seriously, or even know it.

Of course, there may be a few folks that are aware of this scenario. Interestingly, superyacht sales are up 70% from 2021 to 2022, with 900 super yachts sold in that year, But based on the global state of the pyramids, it's safe to say no one knows about the flood coming and that the pyramids are there for us to use for tourism. Did you know they removed a pyramid in Central America to make room for a highway? Just incredible! As I type this, I can imagine the geyser that will be blowing straight up into the sky sometime soon. Humans and their progress, just don't seem to get it. Those in the know are happy to spend untold trillions on trying to get off the planet, but what about the rest of us left here? Could we take

it into our own hands to repair the pyramids
and protect ourselves? YES!

FOLLOW THE CLUES.

Like any good researcher and theoretician, I'm racking my brains for solutions. All the theories that I've read about over the years from Edgar Cayce to Charles Hapgood, Immanuel Velikovsky to Graham Hancock and Randall Carson and everyone in between about extreme earth changes and possible causes of catastrophic floods, leave me still wondering. Some are convinced it's the sun misbehaving; some think it's mega asteroids; some think it's aliens and rogue planets. Everyone knows about the great floods and have theories but none of them seem to fit the total picture as to what causes them and how they happen. The clues are to be found in a few lines from the ancient Sumerian cylinder texts and the Annunaki story, and the Bible texts about the Noah's flood.

The Temple Mount has all the tell-tale signs of being a location of a vent from an underground ocean at one time as there are massive hundred ton stones that make up the foundation of the Temple Mount. Inside the golden Dome of the Rock, rare photos of the interior show us a huge slab of stone with a small hole in it. Beneath this rock, accessed by stairs now, is a large cavern once thought to be a 'cistern' or well. It's all quiet now but was it once fed by a hot water spring – a subdued geyser? There's no doubt in my mind this place might be the place Noah's flood started, which is why it got to be so holy. Could it start from here again? In Revelations, there's talk about the Euphrates and the Tigris rivers drying up. Verses in the Koran talk of the 'end times' being near when water starts to flow 'out of the desert'. Many prophecies are possibly seen happening today, especially in last few decades.

At Baalbek in Lebanon, the stones in the temple there weigh in at 1000 tons: it's quite possible that these enormous buildings are built over hydrothermal vents to check the mega-geysers.

I am writing this to give out as much information as I can on this NFC scenario so you, the concerned, can help humanity get this right. I know I'm on the right track, as I can describe the function of the Great Pyramid of Giza to the point one would struggle to argue against the mechanics and the evidence. That does not mean there won't be a line of people supporting the opposition, lined up down the street and around the corner!

Right now, as previously mentioned, I can honestly say that we could be trapped in a vicious time cycle of only tens-of-thousands of years with continuous ice and water cycles following each other like clockwork. What's scary is that humanity seems to know we are heading towards something big, with all the talk of 'climate change'. Are we to blame – well, yes, especially if we don't do what we can to protect ourselves.

The Jewish Calendar is at year 5783 starting from the year Adam and Eve came onto the scene. Did humanity have to start again after the world was 'washed clean' only 6 thousand years ago? And is the world becoming 'wicked and degenerate' a sign that God would want to wash it clean again? Look around you, folks…

It makes sense looking at the geological time for the water cycle to complete, that the NFC happens at the height of man's climb to the pinnacle of material and social achievements in that cycle.

Just amazing no one has taken the flood stories serious enough to figure out where the source of Noah's flood waters come from? Even the name No and Ah - sounds one would make within this time of deluge!

To reiterate what the global pyramids were originally built for, the pyramids were built to stop these huge hydrothermal high pressure water and steam mega-geysers from gushing into the atmosphere by keeping this steam and water flow on the ground and channel it into a nearby river or nearby ocean to condense and cool unwanted hydrothermal water/steam exhaust from the upper mantle.

The Great Pyramid of Giza is the smoking gun in my catalogue of evidence, where one can explain the entire working of the Great Pyramid of Giza. The facts are, we collectively are in denial of anything about this water cycle that has been plaguing every form of life on the planet.

PHILOSOPHICAL THOUGHTS

Now let's speak philosophically about this divine design built by the gods. Obviously humans and many other forms of life on Earth do get out of balance and out of order on the planet and destroy other forms of life. These human life forms also destroy the very habitats and the environment that support life as we know it. If the two shutting-down mechanisms were not in place (the ice age and the water age) the planet's life-giving environment would eventually be destroyed by the planet itself continually heat up. This is a likely answer to what happened to Mars, and our Moon. . One can imagine that Martians went horribly wrong and messed up their planetary protection system on Mars and destroyed their planet Mars for good.

We must give thanks for the "Thermostat Creator and the Technology of the Gods"

There is a fine line to be drawn, between allowing things to happen naturally and, as intelligent beings, we do not derail this divine thermostat set up to protect the planet

There is no doubt in my mind that the &%$#@!- up system or power we have on Earth now would try to stop this divine planetary shut down system for a profit without blinking an eye, which begs the question? Why even inform humanity about it?

Am I the first human being in our time to actually figure out what the pyramids are built for? Is it my ego that gets excited by this revelation? Is it the thought of making a load of big bucks? (That would be nice!)

Is it fame? (Ooh the fame could be fun and entertaining), but that's not it either.

I'll tell you what it is: it's this notion that I believe in humanity to do the right thing, to lower the loss of life, pain and suffering for all species on the planet that drives my will to turn this over to the Human family.

EARLY SIGNS

Is it possible that the Temple Mount is a location that first starts to show water coming up from the ground as a flood warning? The Mount on which Solomon's Temple once stood has channels and tunnels through which fresh water flows. There is an account of water flowing from the 'stones' of the temple, of water flowing **up** to the top level where Solomon's Temple once stood, a sign which became known as the 'Precursor to the appearance of the Messiah'. (Messiah? Or Flood?)

Every temple on Earth is situated over a natural source of water, for many reasons. One being to watch when the fountains of the deep start to rise.

An Islam prophet predicted that one of the signs of Judgment Day would be that the land of Arabia would return to greenery and rivers, as it once was. Well, (pun intended!) don't look now because water is coming out of the ground in this desert as we speak, creating a river. This, to me, makes sense as the subterranean freshwater oceans must be close to being filled to capacity and this is why we will see more and more new sources of freshwater coming up out of the ground. Also, we will find more and more temporary surface flash floods, as the deep water table rises closer to the surface. Where can water run to, now?

SHELL HASH EVIDENCE

Flood Paleontology (the study of fossils formed in the flood) is a science which studies the species that became extinct during floods. Comparing scientific studies of fossils with scripture's narrative of the flood, we notice the flood accounts tell us about the destruction of life:

"And all flesh died that moved upon the earth, both of fowl, and of cattle, and of beast, and of every creeping thing that creepeth upon the earth, and every man: All in whose nostrils was the breath of life, of all that was in the dry land, died." Genesis Ch 8: v 21-22.

Fossils are a very rare occurrence on earth, they are so rare because of the absolute pristine untouched environment that must stay untouched for an incredible huge amount of time, coupled with how rare it is for an environment to exist undisturbed right after the death of a species, because earth has the best clean up system for the dead: scavengers, bacteria and just the natural weather with rain and the hot sun alone will disintegrate almost anything in a very short amount of time. For most fossils to be created, the creature needs to die in shallow water where sediment covers the remains that make which then may up a clay or sedimentary rock like limestone all the while the remains must not be disturbed while the entombing process continues.

The book of Genesis and the epic of Gilgamesh both have similar flood stories. Scholars attribute this worldwide flood occurrence as nothing more than 'good ol' storytelling around the campfire', but recently, around the world, many paleontologists and scientists are finding evidence of recurrent worldwide floods.

One site has uncovered evidence of Noah's Flood in an astonishing site near the Black Sea some 7500 years ago. *Glaciers* flowed out of the Black Sea basin into the Mediterranean Sea, which is connected to the Atlantic Ocean. At some point in time, the flow was reversed and the Mediterranean Sea started to flow north into the Black Sea, which was quite a bit lower. Dozens of feet below the present seafloor off the coast of Crimea, core samples were taken in layered mud. Carbon dating of shells in this mud indicates that it was laid down between 18000 and 8600 years ago. Directly above the layers of mud is a layer called 'shell hash', an inch thick layer of broken shells, overlain by several feet of fine sediment of the type being brought into the Black Sea by rivers today. The shells in the hash are typical of what was in the Black Sea when it was a body of *fresh* water. The fine sediments contain evidence of *salt* water species, previously unknown in the Black Sea.

It is the interpretation of these layers that tells us what happened on the inevitable day at the bottom of the Bosporus when all hell broke loose.

When the Mediterranean began to flow northward, the incoming water dug a channel 300 feet deep as it poured into the Black Sea basin, changing it from a freshwater lake to a saltwater ocean (which, by the way, I had the pleasure of sailing through courtesy of the US Navy, with port of calls in Romania and Istanbul, Turkey).

In this scenario, the mud beneath the shell hash represents sediment from the rivers that fed the freshwater lake flowing towards a saltwater ocean. The shell hash above the sediment is from the remains of water creatures that lived in that lake, and the layers *above* the shell hash were the result of seawater incursion.

This event could have been the flood recorded in the book of Genesis. The volume of water flowing *into* the Black Sea could be comparable to 200 times the water volume flowing over Niagara Falls. Now imagine that scale of water movement happening around the world, where the waters 'from the deep' cause these enormous water flows.

Archaeologists propose that the flood displaced a lot of people and actually caused the break-up of the Indo-European language that split up before 3500 BCE - after the Black Sea flood event.

The other evidence we see is the settlement of people after the flood, which shows not one of them is less than 150 feet above sea level, suggesting that these people thought that this flood might happen again.

GLOBAL FLOOD GEOLOGY

"Researcher and scientists Michael J. Oard uses his knowledge of the Ice Age and Missoula Flood to lay out his case for a Global Flood. He shares how many geologic features on the surface of the earth just can't be explained through slow and gradual processes, but rather, one worldwide Flood. These features include water and wind gaps, the continental shelves, submarine canyons, planation surfaces, pediments, and the spread of exotic rocks. His convincing evidence will challenge conventional thinking, showing how the biblical record makes much more sense of the evidence."

You Tube video.
Flood Geology | Episode 4 | The Receding Floodwaters | Michael J. Oard

GODS INSTRUCTIONS TO NOAH

Let's talk more about the Noah time and the ark being a pyramid in the Dead Sea scrolls. Let's imagine God's conversation with Noah.

"Noah!"
"Yes lord!"
 "I need you to build an ark" (or pyramid over a hydro-thermal vent?)"
"Okay, no problem my Lord! Where and how big?"
"450ft x 90ft x 50ft high."(The dimension of the ark).

This rectangular construction could be compared with the Ziggurat at Ur, located between the Tigris and Euphrates, approximately where Noah lived back then.

The one we see today measures 170ft x 125ft x 100ft high.

Building huge constructions were not unusual.

PYRAMIDS and PYRAMID GRAVITY FORCE (PGF)

Magma and/or water?

It makes more sense to me, after putting the big picture together, the true purpose of the pyramids. Let's reiterate exactly what a pyramid is built and used for:

In essence, as stated earlier, some pyramids are giant corks using their shear mass and weight to stop the subterranean water geysers flowing up from the Earth's mantle. The more sophisticated pyramid, the Great Pyramid of Giza, is a very complex pyramid that can handle the high temperature flows and pressure and divert this flow out a swinging six ton stone check valve door when the pressure gets too high.

Now, that being said, the two pyramids that are missing did not have the engineering technology and possibly just got destroyed from the inside and the remainder of the stones like I said earlier were hauled off by camels to build Cairo.

My initial theory on the pyramids proposed that they controlled the gravitational field between the Earth and Moon to counter-balance magma currents and lock magnetic north into true north. This doesn't negate that they also control water flow from the deep Transition Zone from where the mega-geysers originate. It all works together in geo-engineering technology. The very fact that these pyramids still stand today stand as testimony that someone, sometime had that technology.

I formulated a gravity theory based on my observations that all the large pyramids align with a volcano 180 degrees opposed to each other, on the same approximate longitude and latitude lines" The gravity theory is a displacement theory and a commonsense theory with other physical repeatable evidences. For instance, did you know that every continent aligns with a sister continent? Asia/America; Australia/South America; Antarctica/Arctic; Hawaii (Pacific)/Africa. (This is still unbeknownst to mainstream theoretical geophysics).

I'm thinking what might be happening now is that the pyramids on the Giza plateau are lowering the gravitational field under the Hawaiian 'hotspot' allowing magma to flow out of the Hawaiian hotspot, making it a constantly erupting volcano in a class of its own, that defies explanation to this day - apart from that it is a slowly moving open volcanic vent on the Pacific floor, which has made the Hawaiian Archipelago above sea-level.

The Hawaiian 'hotspot', otherwise known as the Kilauea Volcano on Big Island, Hawaii, rises 4000 feet above sea level and is constantly active, thus lowering the gravitational field 180 degrees to the east, and west, on the same approximate latitude, where we find the Great Pyramids on the Giza plateau, the volcano lowers the gravitational fields under Giza that allows underground oceans to expand overtime.

Both magma and water are managed in a geo-thermal technology, and so my Pyramid Gravity Theory is still somewhat intact.

Hawaii is not a continent but when the sea levels drop again there will be many land masses in the Pacific Ocean floor that will be exposed above water again, which will align with Africa.

I guess what I'm trying to point out here is that gravity has a self-balancing mechanism which we see throughout the universe. Every large mass eventually takes up a spherical shape especially if it is hot and molten. This is due to gravity displacement. In the beginning of Earth's creation, the planet was just covered with water with no visible land. Then the Earth went into its first ice age: huge ice glaziers rose up to the heavens (where North America is today). Following the gravitational theory, where balance occurs 180 degrees on the same longitude, or latitude, opposite North America, we find the Himalayas.

Now, as Earth goes into its first interglacial period the glaciers begin to, then eventually completely melt.

The Himalayas lower the gravitational field, 180 degrees opposite, and allow the Sierra Nevada, the Rocky Mountains, and the Appalachian Mountain Range to rise and balance out the Earth.

We see the same gravitational activity with a moon high tide and a moonless high tide on the opposite side of the planet, every day.
In essence, the moon pulls the Earth's gravitational field towards it thus lowering the gravitational field 180 degrees opposed to it, allowing the ocean to rise on the moonless side of the planet. (I've tried to get this published for peer review and hired a physicist with tenor at an American university. Well, as you can imagine we were

like oil and water! We could not agree on anything! I get it - my theories fly in the face of a hundred years of physics theory and as he said, "Your hypothesis and equations don't align with any *known* science of the day". (By far the best compliment anyone in explorative research physics could receive, ha-ha!).

The other problem he had was that the *Pangea* theoretical scenario is destroyed by my gravity theory as there can be no 'continental drift' at all. I guess theoretical geophysics is not ready for me.

But who knows, maybe some time in the future they will have to throw some accepted theories out the window when it doesn't add up mathematically. That has happened before, but the established school of thought stubbornly holds on to what has been established. That said, I supply much physical evidence to back up my theories.

Building huge pyramids is for stopping the flow of steam and water from discharging directly into the atmosphere causing instantaneous climate disruption and destroying local habitats and global environments

If you look at the location of these large Giza pyramids, you can see the urgency to manage the extreme discharges of water to protect life: a large population and the farmland that fed it. Egypt is a country that grew and evolved from the eco-system alongside a life-giving river – the Nile.

We can now solve the age old conundrum of why the Sphinx enclosure has water erosion all around it. It was a tank, or reservoir, or hot spa, for the use of the privileged people of Memphis, later called Cairo.

DIVINE INSTRUCTIONS

Just as our hero, Noah, had his instructions to build his huge house-boat, so did his descendants get their instructions to build huge pyramids - one in particular to a high technical specification - to control a dormant hydrothermal vent that could soon be blowing millions of gallons of super-heated water all over the ancient cities, causing a flood and basically destroying all the palaces, temples, homes and farms in the immediate area.

WORLD PYRAMIDS

Ziggurat of Ur.

One 'cradle of civilization' is where the first city of modern man is said to have been built. It is known as Ur in Sumer, Mesopotamia, home of the Anunnaki clay tablets and some of the earliest forms of cuneiform writing and incredible art. We can see the urgency for building a pyramid in this location! I guess the same can be said for South and Central America, China and Egypt. Most of these huge pyramid building sites were home to, or still are, places where large populations live. Some have been captured by the jungles of South America and are hidden now.

An enormous 'White Pyramid' (above) near the Chinese city of Xi'an, is said to have been seen by a pilot during a flight between India and China during World War II, who described it as a 'white jewel-topped pyramid'. Not only was this extraordinary structure said to be the largest pyramid in the world but, in the valleys surrounding it, there were said to be dozens of other pyramids, some rising to an elevation almost as great. The Chinese have recently planted thousands of trees on their pyramids so tourists and possible treasure hunters can't see or find them.

Officials claim they are waiting until technology advances enough to properly excavate the pyramids and their precious contents. After all, some of the pyramids are believed to date as far back as 8,000 years. (anomalien.com)

Many of these pyramids are earthen pyramids with huge boulders and horizontal plates made out of other materials. I guess having plants growing on the outside of the pyramids would actually increase the overall strength of the pyramid. Is it possible somebody in China knows more about the purpose of the pyramids than they are telling the world?

DAMAGED and DANGEROUS

The Great Pyramid of Giza gifts us a historical database that can be accessed once we figure out the design concept, and that design concept is to withstand extreme internal pressures in excess of 3000 psi with a higher maximum of perhaps 10000 psi. Another clue is the three 'girdle stones' on the ascending passageway: these stones are solid square stone with a smaller square cut right out of the middle weighing in at 5000 pounds. The ascending passageway goes right through these girdle stones.

If we look at these extreme pressures that the pyramid is designed to operate at, a girdle stone is used to stop any external bulging movements of the ascending passageway.

In other words, this is another smoking gun pointing to the fact that the pyramid is designed to withstand extreme high pressure from within, caused by the super-heated water and steam coming from the Transition Zone below the Earth's crust.

Another way of looking at the girdle stone is this: it was used like a regular hose clamp; one tightens the clamp to stop a leak on the hose. A wooden barrel has metal bands around it to keep a keg of spirits from blowing up when internal pressures rise from fermentation.

There are also many of these girdle stones, some 20 in all, on the passageway leading up towards the main entrance, which makes sense because the closer you get to the outer casing of the pyramid the less structural strength the passageway has from the surrounding stones of the pyramid. In other words, the chambers and passageways are reinforced by the high number of stones and shear mass weight the closer you get to the centerline of the pyramid.

The Great Pyramid of Giza needs a lot of work to be done – ASAP! I would not want to live in Cairo when the super-heated high pressure water supply from the Transition Zone decides to vent again.

Moving to the upper section of the GP1 design we see that the 'Relieving Chambers' have a vertical tunnel, hand dug, to enter these 5 chambers. The first or lowest one is called the 'Davidson Tunnel'

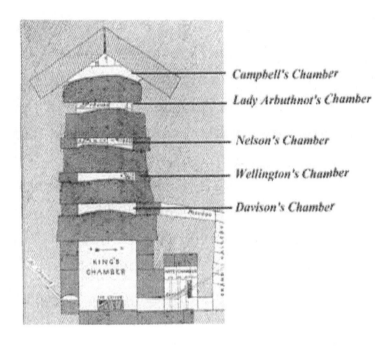

Campbell's Chamber

Lady Arbuthnot's Chamber

Nelson's Chamber

Wellington's Chamber

Davison's Chamber

As seen in the drawing above, it shows all the tunneling from the King's chamber up to the Davidson chamber, then the tunneling into the above four chambers all of which compromises the design.

Ideally, if you don't know what it does, put it back the way you found it!

The so-called 'Al-Mamun's entrance' is **wide open**; both King and Queen's chambers are **wide open**, along with the two air vents in both chambers. As I keep stressing, all the pyramids are **wide open** because of exploration and damage caused from looters and archaeologists, historians and tourism. Pyramids were built to protect Man and all other life species on Earth and they have all now been turned into amusement parks.

Here is the promise of the top management of the pyramid construction company:

11 "And I will establish my covenant with you; neither shall **all** flesh be cut off any more by the waters of a flood; **and henceforth there shall be no flood to destroy the Earth.**" Genesis Ch 9: v 11

Okay, the key word here is **all** and he didn't destroy the Earth, either. The planet was washed clean and renewed, but life on it perished. And it is evident that God didn't destroy **all** last time. It is evident that there were survivors, maybe not just Noah and his ark full of family and animals.

There have been pyramid researchers who have focused on the function of water. Some, I can't go along with, but the 'evaporator/cooling' guys who came up with a bicarbonate theory to pump water was quite genius and their work on the girdle blocks runs with my theory also.

REVELATIONS

Flood prophecy or history?
Kingjamesbibleonline.org/Revelation

One flood was not so big and soon drained away.

15 "And the serpent **cast out of his mouth water as a flood** after the woman, that he might cause her to be carried away of the **flood**.
16 "And the earth helped the woman, and the **earth opened her mouth, and swallowed up the flood** which the dragon cast out of his mouth."
Revelations Ch 12: v 15, 16

In Revelations, we come to read of all hell breaking loose, the destruction of Mount Geddon or Megiddo, aka **Armageddon**, an important city on a 3-way trade route (in Israel), where demons and angels cause heaven and earth to break apart in a huge earthquake with electric storms and huge hailstones. And those in Babylon saw and were warned.

16 "And he gathered them together into a place called in the Hebrew tongue Armageddon.

17 "And the seventh angel poured out his vial into the air; and there came a great voice out of the temple of heaven, from the throne, saying, 'It is done'.

18 "And there were voices, and thunders, and lightning; and there was a great earthquake, such as was not since men were upon the earth, so mighty an earthquake, and so great.

19 "And the great city was divided into three parts, and the cities of the nations fell: and great Babylon came in remembrance before God, to give unto her the cup of the wine to the fierceness of his wrath.

20 "And every island fled away, and the mountains were not found.

21 "And there fell upon men a great hail out of heaven, every stone about the weight of a talent: and men blasphemed God because of the plague of

the hail; for the plague thereof was exceeding great."
Rev: Ch16: v 16-21

The vision then showed John (the Divine, not John the Shaughnessy) looking down on Jerusalem, which shone like a jewel. But then he saw a new city, with dimensions of a **pyramid**!

3 'gates' (triangular) on each of its 4 sides, 12 'gates' in all, oriented to east, north, south and west, and it was measured with a 'golden reed' (designed on the Golden Mean) and it was '4-square' with a circumference of 12000 furlongs, each wall 144 cubits, and it shone gold, like pure glass.

(The Giza pyramids were cased in smooth stone and could be seen shining brightly from a great distance. It is also thought that they were surrounded by water).

10 "And he carried me away in the spirit to a great and high mountain, and shewed me that great city, the holy Jerusalem, descending out of heaven from God,

11 "Having the glory of God: and her light was like unto a stone most precious, even like a jasper stone, clear as crystal;

12 "And [the new city] had **a wall great and high,** and had **twelve gates,** and at the gates twelve angels, and names written thereon, which are the names of the twelve tribes of the children of Israel:

13 "**On the east three gates [triangular]; on the north three gates; on the south three gates; and on the west three gate**s.

14 "And the wall of the city had **twelve foundations** [4sided pyramids x 3], and in them the names of the twelve apostles of the Lamb.

15 "And he that talked with me had a **golden reed** to measure the city, and the gates thereof, and the wall thereof.

16 "And the city lay **four-square,** and the **length is as large as the breadth**: and he measured the city with the **reed, twelve thousand furlongs**. The

length and the breadth and the height of it are equal [pyramidal].

17 "And he measured the wall thereof, an **hundred and forty and four** cubits, according to the measure of a man, that is, of the angel.

18 "And the building of the wall of it was of jasper: and the city was **pure gold, like unto clear glass.**

19 "And the foundations of the wall of the city were garnished with all manner of precious stones. The first foundation was jasper; the second, sapphire; the third, a chalcedony; the fourth, an emerald;

20 "The fifth, sardonyx; the sixth, sardius; the seventh, chrysolite; the eighth, beryl; the ninth, a topaz; the tenth, a chrysoprasus; the eleventh, a jacinth; the twelfth, an amethyst [all the colors of a rainbow]

21 "And the twelve gates were twelve pearls; every several gate was of one pearl: and the street of the city was pure gold, as it were transparent glass.

22 "And I saw **no temple** therein: for the Lord God Almighty and the Lamb are the temple of it.

23 "And the city had **no need of the sun, neither of the moon,** to shine in it: for the glory of God did lighten it, and the Lamb is the light thereof.

24 "And the nations of them which are saved shall **walk in the light of it**: and the **kings [pharaohs] of the earth** do bring their glory and honor into it.
25 "And the gates of it shall not be shut at all by day: for there shall be **no night** there.
26 "And they shall bring the glory and honor of the nations into it". Revelations 21:10-26

This was 'no temple' and it shone on its own, without sun or moon to light it (self-illuminating) and people who came afterwards, came to be in its light. The kings (pharaohs) put their names on it (Khufu, Cheops, and Menkaure). It shone continually, day and night. It was one of the 'seven wonders of the world'.

This has to be the Great Pyramids of Giza. What was its power source? Hydro-electric power from the water source beneath? Solar? Free universal energy? Ionization?

On the left above we see the badly damaged and eroded pyramid at Giza (GP2) and on the right we see an artist's impression of how they may have looked in their original, pristine state.

Was Revelation the record of 'God's wrath' and the destruction of the great cities that had become corrupt and degenerate by bringing on Noah's Great Flood to wash their sins away? Is it also a record of how the great cities were rebuilt afterwards, installing pyramids to prevent it happening again? Is it also a warning that if we don't get our act together and prepare for the next one we shall be in dire straits.

The pyramid technology came to intelligent civilizations who worked out how to watch for the early signs of the next flood coming and get on with building the huge pyramids over the most potentially dangerous geyser vents around the world? Did they also protect exhausted vents with temples, megalithic to start with then architecturally designed temples, to bring people to pray and ask for guidance and protection from any future destruction?

Perhaps all the world's sacred sites were part of a global system of early-warning, protection and geo-engineering to keep this planet we call home safe to live in.

The angels or demons exhausted the wrath of the fountains of the deep in the land of Adam and Eve, the original Garden of Eden, where Noah built a ziggurat (somehow translated to, or associated with the word ark) to stop or slow down the flooding and build a safe haven while the waters rose, so his offspring could survive along with many living animals.

As I type this the news is full of battles raging on this Earth with humans trying to kill humans as fast as possible in wars, and other groups crying out the 'climate-change' message, and others optimistically trying to get us off fossil fuels and to 'go green'. It's a mad shouting match of crazy people all knowing something and trying to do something, but it's chaotic and not getting us anywhere good.

What if we all calmed down and focused our attention on rebuilding and repairing our best safety valves – the pyramids.

TIMES AND DATES

"Genesis 6—9 records the events of Noah's flood, also called the Great Flood. If the genealogy provided in Genesis 5 is intended to be comprehensive, we can determine the dates of various events by simply adding up the time spans between fathers and sons, given in Genesis 5:

Adam	to	Seth	—	130	years
Seth	to	Enosh	—	105	years
Enosh	to	Kenan	—	90	years
Kenan	to	Mahalalel	—	70	years
Mahalalel	to	Jared	—	65	years
Jared	to	Enoch	—	162	years
Enoch	to	Methuselah	—	65	years
Methuselah	to	Lamech	—187		years
Lamech	to	Noah	—182		years

According to this method, the time from Adam to Noah was approximately 1056 years. These are approximate times because we don't know if the years are counted from conception or birth; also, it is obvious that the years are given in whole numbers but no doubt included (or excluded) partial years. (For instance, Adam was 130 years old when Seth was born, give or take a certain number of months and days.)

So we have Noah's birth, which occurred about 1,056 years after the creation of Adam. Then, in Genesis 7:11, we are told that the flood came in the 600th year of Noah's life, so that would mean the Great Flood came approximately 1,656 years after Adam was created in Eden. Using a similar method places the creation of Adam and Eve at around 4004 BC. So, doing the math, **Noah's flood occurred in approximately**

2348BC.

Similar genealogies are found throughout the Old Testament. Using the same method places Abraham's calling at 228 years after Noah's flood or about 1,884 years after the dawn of humanity.

We can also use the genealogies to count backward from other dates that we know, such as the fall of Jerusalem. Using this method, Abraham was born about 2166 BC, and the exodus during Moses' time would have happened about 446BC.

Some scholars believe that the genealogies are not intended, and were never understood by the original audience, to be exhaustive. It could be that generations were skipped, as we know happened in the genealogy of Jesus recorded in Matthew. If this is the case in the Genesis 5 genealogy, and there are years

unaccounted for, then **we really have no idea when the Great Flood took place**".
gotquestions.org/

SOME WORD CONNECTIONS

In Thessalonians Ch 2, the bible says that this 'man' is to be revealed in his time when the thing that is restraining him on Earth is removed or lifted; he is the man of 'Sin'.' When the fullness of iniquity fills the 'cup' to the point of running over this is when God makes his judgment. Every time I see the word 'cup', I think about the Holy Grail.

'Sin' is the ancient name for the Moon, and we know the Moon has significant gravitational influence on Earth's water. (See our book 'There Is Something About The Moon')

In Genesis the world was covered in water. When God's 'hand' is on the Earth, he divides the firmament in two creating the upper and lower mantle and the Transition

Zone forms, allowing ocean levels to fall, as the Transition Zone fills, and land to rise. The reverse happens when the 'cup' is full i.e. the underground oceans are full to capacity. God then removes his 'hand' and the firmament becomes one again and the underground ocean rises through the Earth's crust and submerges the land in a great flood, covering all the land and mountains.

Roy Schnyder's quote from the movie Jaws "You're gonna need a bigger boat" comes to mind.

THE FLOOD BEFORE NOAH'S FLOOD

From the Epic of Gilgamesh, in the land of Sumer, we find an original version of the flood.

Noah's biblical deluge story is not original, in fact the Hebrew scholars who were the authors of the Bible accredit the deciphering of 'the 11th tablet' - the Sumerian epoch of Gilgamesh.

According to George Smith at the British Museum, the Babylonian deluge myth originates from Sumerian mythology. In 1872 he was working on a fragment of cuneiform clay text from Nineveh when he suddenly saw the account of a flood identical to Noah's Flood.

The full fascinating account of **George Smith's** discovery, its implications and a full translation of the flood text can be found here:

segulamag.com/en/articles/babylonian-deluge/

Arno Poebel (1881–1958) was a German Assyriologist. In 1905/6, he worked with Sumerian documents at the University of Pennsylvania submitting an edition of Sumerian legal documents as his dissertation in 1906, editing further Sumerian texts during 1912 to 1914. Among his most important finds was discovering and translating the flood story of the Sumerian creation myth in the collection of cuneiform tablets recovered from Sippur which were stored at the University of Pennsylvania. This tablet, dated from c.1700-1600 BC, is the earliest known version of the various forms of flood myth from Mesopotamia. His Sumerian grammar (1923) was seminal to the field of Sumerology and remains relevant.

Poebel immigrated to the United States in 1928, becoming professor of Assyriology and Sumerology at the University of Chicago until his retirement in 1946. (Wiki/edited)

A lone tablet containing the contents of a flood episode is notable just because of the account of the flood episode; it is primarily about **floods**. There are no other deluge tablets nor fragments to be found in any museum, known private collection, or archaeological record anywhere on Earth. This one surviving partial tablet gives us evidence of a flood record before Noah's Flood appeared in the bible.

These texts contain several telling statements concerning the creation of man, the origin of kingship, and the existence of at least five prehistoric cities.

The entire extant text of the myth, includes tantalizing uncertainties. No date can be given for the appearance of these myths.

There is a break of about 37 lines in the lower third of the preserved tablet. A deity then addresses other deities, declaring that he will save humanity from extinction and that, as a result, man will construct the cities and temples of the gods. The address is followed by three lines that describe the deity's action to make his words effective but are hard to put in context. Four more lines follow, beginning with the creation of man, animals, and plants. Overall, it reads like this:

"I will destroy my humankind in its destruction. I will return the people to their homes; they will build the divine laws, and I will comfort them with my shades. Their bricks will be laid in pure places for our houses. Places of purity will be the places of our decisions."

There was a pure fire quenching the water. Rituals were perfected, and divine laws were exalted. He accomplished this on Earth, he put the law in place, then the Earth sprouted lush vegetation after An, Enlil, Enki, and Ninhursag fashioned the black-headed people, and creatures with four legs of the plain were created. We learn that the kingship was lowered from heaven, and five cities were established, by perfecting the rites and the exalted divine laws.

The gods decide to bring the flood and destroy humankind. Some gods are unhappy over the cruel decision. The counterpart to Noah in the bible is Ziusudra. He is a pious, god-fearing king who constantly seeks divine revelations through dreams and incarnations. Ziusudra hears the voice.
Then Ziusudra did giant-size construction,
He acted with humility, obedience and reverence. Constantly attending he brought forth all kinds of dreams. He heard that a flood will destroy the seed of humanity.

This is where the long epic of the Annunaki comes in. The Annunaki were the gods of Sumer and their associations with water run deep!

As it is a huge subject rife with interpretations and theories to the meaning behind this story, I must leave you to do your own research.

Simply put, Enki was a god associated with water and he forewarned Ziusudra (Noah) of the impending flood and wanted to save humanity. Enlil, the brother wanted to destroy humanity. The sister, Ninhursag, or Nanna was the Creatress of the new humanity. The father in heaven was Anu and the Earth was Ki.

Here is a short summary of what is known about the Sumerian gods. (Wiki)

ANNUNAKI

Enki and later Ea were apparently depicted, sometimes, as a man covered with the skin of a fish, and this representation, as likewise the name of his temple E-apsu, "house of the watery deep", points decidedly to his original character as a god of the waters (see Oannes). Around the excavation of the 18 shrines found on the spot, thousands of carp bones were found, consumed possibly in feasts to the god. Of his cult at Eridu, which goes back to the oldest period of Mesopotamian history, nothing definite is known except that his temple was also associated with Ninhursag's temple which was called Esaggila, "the lofty head house" (E, house, sag, head, ila, high; or Akkadian goddess = Ila), a name shared with Marduk's temple in Babylon, pointing to a staged tower or ziggurat (as with the temple of Enlil at Nippur, which was known as E-kur (kur, hill)), and that incantations, involving ceremonial rites in which water as a sacred element played a prominent part, formed a feature of his worship. This seems also implicated in the epic of the 'hieros gamos' or sacred marriage of Enki and Ninhursag (above), which seems an etiological myth of the fertilization of the dry ground by the coming of irrigation water (from Sumerian a, ab, water or semen). The early inscriptions of Urukagina in fact go so far as to suggest that the divine pair, Enki and Ninki, were the progenitors of seven pairs of gods, including Enki as god of Eridu, Enlil of Nippur, and Su'en (or Sin) of Ur, and were themselves the children of An (sky, heaven) and Ki (earth). The pool of the Abzu at the front of his temple was adopted also at the temple to Nanna (Akkadian Sin) the Moon, at Ur, and spread from there throughout the Middle East. It is believed to remain today as the sacred pool at Mosques, or as the holy water font in Catholic or Eastern Orthodox churches.

We find the flood had already raged in all its violence over the land for seven days and nights, as the sun god Atu returns, bringing his precious light everywhere, Ziusudra prostrates himself before him and offers sacrifices. Read the line below:

"Violent windstorms and floods swept over the cult centers after the flood had swept the land for seven days and nights; storms on the mighty waters had tossed the boat about (notice it does not mention ark) He shed light on heaven and earth and Ziusudra opened a window of the vast boat, and Atu (sun) brought his rays back into the giant boat. King Ziusudra slaughters a sheep and an ox."

'Ziusudra was given eternal life when he prostrated himself before An. Enlil was transferred to Dilmun, the city where the Sun rises. Anu and Enlil uttered the breath of heaven and breath of earth and vegetation arises After, Ziusudra, was the keeper of the names of vegetation and the seeds of humankind they caused to dwell in the land of Dilmun, the place where the sun rises".

We now turn to Hades, from Paradise, to the 'mighty below', or as the Sumerians referred to it, 'the land of no return'. This descent to the nether world is one of the best preserved Sumerian myths. A restless goddess descends to the land of the dead to satisfy her unbridled ambitions. This provides a rare parallel with one of the most significant New Testament themes in recent years. Many historical and scriptural findings have been revealed that were not included in or misrepresented in the Canonical bible, historical texts like the Book of Enoch, Nag Hammadi Gospels, and the Book of Jubilees.

With existing documents, they provide a profound understanding of the beliefs shared in modern Western culture. Our knowledge of middle eastern history is enriched by writing that's not part of the Canonical bible. This has had a powerful effect on western thought. In the deserted plains of Mesopotamia lie hidden scrolls in remote caves, cuneiform tablets covered by the sands of time, and monuments aligned perfectly to the solstice and equinoxes. Documents from this period predate the canonical bible by thousands of years; the story's origins and influences are exposed here. Is it surprising to learn that Noah lived in Shuruppak in Sumer.

Summary:

1, the ancient text does talk about the waters coming up from below.

2, the great pyramid, looking through my eyes, and the evidence I present on the design criteria, shows that it was designed to control an enormous volume of water coming up from the Earth's upper mantle. 3, Most pyramids and large earth mounds located around the world are most likely built over these hydrothermal vents.

4, Pyramids, earth mounds, and ziggurats are generally built in close proximity to developed ancient cities.

5, Ancient text tell us that in the end times 150- pound balls of hail fall from the sky.

As an engineer trained in the sciences of thermodynamics, I can see how, having a massive release of hot water blowing hundreds of miles high into the atmosphere, this water with a sudden change in temperature and atmospheric pressure could produce 150 pound balls of hail that would rain down on the local inhabitants and cities and destroy everything above ground.

6, Pyramids, earth mounds, ziggurats and possibly huge stone temples are built to stop uncontrolled discharges of upper and lower water oceans below the Earth's crust from blowing straight up into the atmosphere.

7, now there are uncapped hydrothermal vents, one known as the 'Well from hell' in Beirut, or the well located in Yemen, 100 feet wide and 300 feet deep and is currently dry where the 'djinn' live, another name for demons.

LEFTOVERS

17 "And I saw an angel standing in the sun, who cried in a loud voice to all the birds in midair, 'Come, gather together for the great supper of God, 18 "So that you may eat the flesh of kings, generals, and the mighty, of horses and their riders, and the flesh of all people, free and slave, great and small." Revelations Ch 19: v 17-18

Sounds like an awesome picnic if you're a bird! Obviously, this is the pile of dead carcasses left over when the flood waters recede.

THE BEAST

The Earth has the mark of the beast 666
Earth's orbital speed is 66600 mph around
the sun. We have the proverbial yin and the
yang of Earth, paradise for many and pure
hell for others. That said, the planet is alive.
The continent of Africa is shaped like an
elongated skull and Lake Victoria is
positioned right where the eye is. One has to
look at the total picture to try and get as
much understanding of the world we live in
as possible.

For me I have no problem believing the
Earth can be a beast 666 if it drowns 90
percent of its land life including man and
animals. One has to remove any thought of
narrowing down time lines given from the
ancient texts, clay tablets, Bible and every
other ancient source, because nothing adds
up, literally: people living for 900 hundred

years; Sumerian kings reigning for 200000 years; Adam and Eve come into existence then 1500 years later Noah's flood washes them all away. We have some major, major contradictions with timelines here.

That said, I always knew there was something greater than man that shuts down this life to protect the planet. The Earth is the finest geo-engineered planet in the universe with creation origins rooted in divine design.

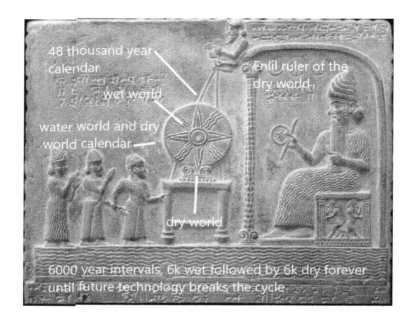

One can see the calendar wheel rotating counter-clockwise. This represents the dividing of the firmament and the merging of the firmament, a cycle of approximately 6 thousand years of the wet world, followed by 6 thousand years of a dry world. The Mayan calendar and yuga cycles operate in the same manner as the above Anunnaki wheel.

It's Becoming abundantly clear that Enki rules the water world, while Enlil rules the dry world, because these images are so profoundly wet and dry. Don't you find the truth is always in plain sight?

CONCLUSION

Here I am in the King's Chamber, going back in time, February 2020, (the very beginning of the global covid 19 shut down!).

As a researcher and scientist I have to recognize the possibility that these pyramids were used when the Earth was in a very different physical state than we observe it today.

That said, common sense in the science of thermodynamics and theoretical geophysics suggest that the ebb and flow of the planet Earth's water system has a built in flood mechanism supplied by an underground anomaly that happens on a very accurate time schedule much like an hourglass filled with sand or ancient water clocks used to tell time. Comparing Europa, a water moon in orbit around planet Jupiter, to a water planet and moon, Earth-and-Moon, is a must when trying to figure out the mechanics of Earth's global flood cycles.

The main difference is Earth has a Transition Zone where Europa does not: the ocean of Europa is in direct contact with the molten mantle of Europa. This leads one to speculate the Earth's ocean floors are not lined with a vinyl liner like a swimming pool! It's pervious with enormous tectonic plate boundaries where water can flow easily down through the upper mantle to the Transition Zone, as stated earlier in this book.

When it comes to the element of water, and in reference to the cyclic floods, "what goes up must come down" and "what goes down must go up", especially when it comes to high temperature upper and lower mantles with a super-heated molten core and internal oceans of water.

For all intent and purposes, Earth is a teapot on the stove, heating water to its boiling point.
Tea anyone?

John Henry Shaughnessy

Tourists having tea on top of the great pyramid in 1938.

Made in the USA
Middletown, DE
06 January 2023